Mea B, a Dubai-based author, has been writing since a very young age. During her long summers in London and countless trips to old bookstores in hidden corners, she found her love for poetry and prose. Most of her writings are inspired from her real-life experiences, but some from movies and books she fell in love with and her wild imagination. Being a writer is one of her many dreams she'd like to accomplish in the future, but it is the closest one to her heart.

To my mother, who got tired of hearing me cry during my heartbreaks and told me to write about it instead.

# MEA B

## ALWAYS ALMOST, UNTIL IT WASN'T

AUSTIN MACAULEY PUBLISHERS™

LONDON • CAMBRIDGE • NEW YORK • SHARJAH

ISBN – 9789948789185– (Paperback)
ISBN – 9789948789192– (E-Book)

Application Number: MC-10-01-6747839
Age Classification: 17+

Printer Name: iPrint Global Ltd
Printer Address: Witchford, England

First Published 2023
AUSTIN MACAULEY PUBLISHERS FZE
Sharjah Publishing City
P.O Box [519201]
Sharjah, UAE
www.austinmacauley.ae
+971 655 95 202

I would like to thank everyone that was with me throughout my writing journey. My mother, a writer herself, who continuously encouraged me to follow my dreams and go out of my way to achieve everything I have ever wished for. My sister and best friends who would always nag me to publish a book so they can brag about being friends with the author. Here we are!

Finally, I'd like to thank the person that most poems are written about; while you caused a lot of heartbreak and pain, you inspired me to write.

# Right Time?

hey
is this the right time?
I've been holding too much in
my emotions are trapped
within my soul, fighting
to blurt out.
please listen…
I'd like your attention;
the pain became unbearable
I don't want to burden you
but I'm tired past the strength
I carried on for too long.
when did you become my nemesis?
my soulmate is long gone
I no longer recognize you
your silence is daunting
what love is this?
this hatred stems from something
somewhere inside of you
confined
in need to see the light
show me your true colors

open your heart to me
I can take it
I promise
I've tolerated your hell
time and time again
and I keep telling myself
manipulators get their way
hypocrites always win
wake up and look around…
it's me and you.
when did differences come between us?
I'm drowning in false hope
clarify us for me
make a decision
wake me up from this nightmare
hey
it's never the right time
but I'm holding too much
and held on too long.

# A Book on a Shelf

I complicated you
you're not hard to read
at all, or understand
the easiest book
I've held
how simple
were the words on your pages
plain words without actions
gray and dull and worthless
I was too complex
my nature was too wild
too alive, too bright
I'm too much for you
of a reader, a woman,
a lover with so much ignition
intelligence and beauty
I was the sun and moon
altogether, I defined the forces
of earth and I combined
heavens together
I am a paradise you dreaded
to understand

I am too much for you
I am irreplaceable
a godsend
I am what never happens
twice, let alone once
I burned you with vividness
suffocated you with attentiveness
and blinded you with love
all whilst you were too easy
too profoundly *idiotic…*
to see me, to appreciate me
you were the scrapings of
love unfound amongst
simplistic books forgotten
in the back of fully stacked
seemingly striking shelves
eye-catching titles
beautiful covers
and empty contents.

you were you…
a book simply too easy
to read
I'd much rather spend
my energy elsewhere.

# Henley on Thames

far off from the noise
the chaos
of what was me and you
the toxicity, the pain
the guilt of who walked away
first and second
and the background
disturbance of anger
of you and I
shouting, arguing,
spiteful words full of
*you*s and *i*s and accusations.

I sat by the river
on the moors and meadows
of Henley on Thames
witnessing a beauty you
won't ever understand
my kind of beauty…
that you never understood.

# You Knew

you knew what you were doing
when you let in a stranger
between us, in our sheets
of betrayal and disloyalty
you knew it would crash
and set fire to our years
and burn and burn and burn
into flames of blames
spitting out venom curses,
striking out each beautiful
memory that seems so far
somehow nonexistent.
you knew what you were doing
so don't blame it on the days
and nights and what ifs and buts…

you knew what you were doing
you knew what you were doing.

and you chose to do it anyway.

# Fake Starlight

maybe it was the fake starlight
I have hung on the walls
of my deserted room
or maybe it was
the scent of your hoodies
perfume and tobacco
or maybe it was
just my bellowing thoughts
screaming your name
drilling it, forcefully
into a life without you.

so many maybes
yet nothing for sure,
except that you're gone
while I'm drowning in cigarettes
red wine and empty sheets.

# Letting You Go

so I sat down by the beach
it was dark, quiet, away from the pier
I could hear the waves hitting the shore
ever so slightly, like a harmony.

and I wanted to think of you
to remember you
but the memories seemed far away
distant
like a distorted mess
fading away
your face seemed unclear
and I forgot the sound of your voice.

I guess, this is moving on
sitting by the beach
and letting you go.

# Stand Tall

like a bird fleeing
from the dangers
of life that burden
my tired little soul
I escape the sorrow
the pain, the cuffs
of the jail-minded trap
I held myself in
I look at myself amongst
the fleeced white-blue
sky, and I lift my head
and drain the tears
you have yourself
so stand tall
and again, I tell myself
so stand tall
you have yourself.

# False Hope

oh, little waves tinkling
under the sun, like stars
on a crystal-clear sky
how peaceful-minded we
were, on a shore-bench
reminiscing, clinging on
endless hope that our
past is relived somehow.

oh, little waves tinkling
under the frowning sun
like gems lost in a sea
of torn emotions…how
wrecked my feelings were
clinging on what we left behind;
the false hope, the aching
memories of you and I.

# Rock-Bottom

rock-bottom, I fall
unconsciously into
what seemed like
a heavenly fantasy
glistening shades of
bright rainbows surrounding
my heart with compassion;
*heaven*, I wondered…
until dark skies, vicious waves
brutally washed away my
picturesque rainbows
throwing me off to
a cold-hearted shore.

love and happiness aren't
roses and sunshine; my dear
love pains, suffers and kills
your young soul with no mercy.

# Ultimate Codependency

blindfolded, I roamed
within, your blood-red
veins that imprisoned
me without exposure.

it was your eyes that saw
your air I breathed, the
ultimate codependency
that kept me alive.

it was you I owed life to
it was you that fed me
love, desire and yet…
it was you that slit the vein.

blindfold's off, exposed
here I am, to the world;
it's my eyes that envision, air
through my lungs that breathe.

it's me relying on me
it's me…keeping me alive.

# Halfway

"meet me halfway,"
you said last winter
as we sealed our goodbye
in a kiss of hope
we'd be reunited one day.

platform 6, today
a suitcase in one hand
a train ticket
clenching my jaws
wiggling my toes
under my rain boot
nervous I was
to see you again.

you see
I've never been to Liverpool
or traveled miles
for someone before
I thought we'd be a mere
idea of a winter fling.

here you are
a big grin
a tight hug
as you embraced my arrival;
"I met you halfway."

# **Just Another London Trip**

two am flight to Heathrow
yet another winter
Christmas, new year
spent away from home
what's new?
running away from troubles
and misery
of being imprisoned of my dauntless nature
it wasn't rainy, unlike the usual
gray skies of London
or foggy
clear as my mind, that first
inhale of fresh air.

ten pm walk in Sloane
Christmas Eve, bright lights
empty streets
carrying my heavy heart
to you
walked past our spot
where we fell in love…
and drifted apart.

twelve am, New Year's Eve,
countdowns and couples
packed streets
profound fireworks of hope
I have finally decided its time
for a resolution
a new beginning;
a life without you.

# Different Forms of Love

love comes in different forms;
you get the love that makes you adore life
see sunshine and rainbows
and a love that kills your soul.

my luck gave me the second one.

I loved you so fiercely
a love so raw and strong
that shook the world. I loved
your demons and danced with them
celebrating agony and pain
in a hell of mistrust
lies and cheating and restless nights.

I loved your manipulative nature
that shackled me into the
deepest depths of aching desire.

I loved you, regardless,
and if loving you meant hell
I was ready to fight, burn
and die for it.

# Summer Fling

you didn't catch my eye…at first
the day I first saw you at the café
I wasn't even paying attention to
my friends, when they nudged me,
"he's checking you out." and I shrugged.
I took your number for the fun of it
*let's have a summer fling,* I thought
*probably won't even last long, a week or so.*
and we went out, how heavenly your scent was
when I hugged you and my face buried in
your neck…and I inhaled my muse
and we had coffee, and talked
for what seemed like forever
we laughed a lot, you sparked something in me
that died a long time ago
and I fell in love right then and there
the heaviness of my heart the next day
when I hugged you goodbye
as you were leaving to the airport
and I told you, please, don't let this be a fling
don't let it be temporary
don't forget me, don't ignore my texts

don't treat me like everyone does
don't let go
"I'd never," you said to my ear, and let go
of our hug to walk out the door, and

I reached out to your hands, pulled you
back in my arms, praying to god
that this is where you'll always be.

# Broken

it's been two months and yet
the days without you still
feel long and heavy
it feels hard to breathe
to eat, to live
to move on
I can't.
I can't walk a step away
from you, from us
what we were. I can't
breathe without your air
in my lungs, your blood
in my veins, I can't function
without your voice
in the back of my head
without your name in my heart
the world feels unbearable,
I have no faith left, or desire
to wake up yet another day
doubt everyone's intention
or their claims of loving me

questioning loyalties and faithfulness

you broke me.

# I Miss You

I miss you
I really do
and sometimes, I forget
how I'm supposed to
breathe
now that you're gone.

the world feels
heavy
and empty
and sometimes
it feels like it ended
most days
I stay up thinking
about you
and us
and her in between
the way you left
the words you said
the words unsaid
the way you
tossed me

like I mean nothing
like I meant nothing
like we were nothing
and I ask myself
why
how
when
did everything crash
and burn
and turn to hell?
how did you
us, a heaven
tear
and shatter
and why did everything
end the way it did?

I miss you
I really do
and sometimes, I forget
how I'm supposed to
live
now that you're gone.

# Absent

I don't know how I got here
how I drifted onto
this rocky shore
of pain and mistrust
of hurt and misery
I don't know how
life unfolded into this
hurricane, this disaster
I don't know how you
left me for her
after nine long years
of so-called love
was it actually?
or was it oblivion
that I chose to live in
and feel and breathe?
I don't know how you
can walk away hand in hand
with her, disregarding
my existence, completely
constantly?

and here I thought
after nine long years
I was your soulmate.

# Purity

immortalized, we lay
on bedsheets of purity
your hands cuffing my cheeks
my hands on your chest.

I felt the rapid beating
of that organ embraced within
speaking the letters
of my name, with every breath.

It was a holy night where
I gave in to your needs…and mine
where we became one
our bodies intertwined.

my virtue now gone
my heart…absent
I am left bare, miserable
hugging endless bloodied sheets.

not everything is meant to be
sometimes, we have to fight against our odds.

# The Reality

Yes, losing you hurt. but it isn't what killed me.

It's after you were gone that I was devoured in pain, it's when during the day I forget we aren't together and I reach for my phone, wanting to call to ask where you were…and then realize I'm not meant to do that…we aren't together anymore.

It's when I smell your perfume randomly and I look all around the place, hoping it was you wearing that scent, it's when I look for your face among a crowd, hoping, just hoping I'd see you again.

It's when I check my phone constantly for a message from you, an email, a missed call…anything, just anything.

It's when it rains and I'm driving around and your song comes on and I look to my right and I see a ghost of you.

It's when I hear her name and wonder why I wasn't good enough.

It's when I do my makeup and tears come pouring out and I cancel my plans and hide in my bed, avoiding life.

It's when I lost my appetite because food became a luxury I no longer had.

It's when I thought overdosing on drugs would lessen my pain.

It's when I wake up from a nightmare and I head to the bathroom to cry on the cold hard floor.
It's when I sit down for hours, writing letters for you that I know you'll never read.

It's when reality slaps my face that you're no longer mine.

# Here's to Us Coming to an End

Growing up together, witnessing each other graduating high school, waving our goodbyes when I left for university abroad…the arguments, the long distance, the breakups every few months just to come back running to each other, and then I came back and we picked up from where we left off, just to realize that a lot had changed.

The growing apart, the learning of what makes us, us. The sudden want of different things, the new interests, the new routines, the little changes of personality, the heightened sense of freedom and the emergence of the new us, the realistic version of us, the us who figured themselves out.

Yet we hung on, loved each other no matter the changes and despite the struggle to accept them. We fought against it all, we remained together when everyone thought it was a ticking time bomb that will set off and set us apart. But, we couldn't. We couldn't let go.

Until one day, we were forced to, one day it was all too much, too real. The arguments became unforgivable, the words were too hurtful and the actions were intolerable. One day, what was okay was not, the things we loved about each other became the same things we hated.

What happened to us? Did we go against normality? Did our love always have an expiration date that we were too oblivious to know about? Did we have too much faith that nothing could break us?

Or was it just the end…the end that had to happen. The end that shatters everything, finally caught up on us and now it was our turn to taste the bitterness of it?

# A Letter Unsent

Hi,

I can't remember the last time I had the urge to let out my feelings for you. For so long, I thought everything inside of me died and I guess I kinda died somehow too. The world felt flat when you left. The air was the same but it was harder to inhale, the sun stopped shining bright enough and the night seemed haunted by my demons.

Everything turned darker.

The world, my soul and most of my heart too.

I guess it's because I nearly died when you left, actually nearly died. After I found out about you and her, I hit rock-bottom. I thought dying was my only escape, so I raided the medicine drawer and the next thing I knew, I was in a train station in a foreign country laying on the floor with my eyes rolling back and my sister trying to keep me awake.

I remember thinking that if I just let go…if I just stop resisting, I will be gone. I thought an eternal hell would be a lot like my reality. I was so ready to just leave this world for you and her and a thousands of her. I was ready to leave the disappointment and pain. I wanted to let go so badly but I couldn't. All I could hear in my head was Mom crying and praying that she doesn't lose her daughter to some guy who failed to love her.

I wish I could tell you that this shit-show I'm putting on for you to see how much I'm *living my life* was real. It started as a coping mechanism, where I would purposely get out of my comfort zone to attempt at moving on, but then it turned into a war between me and you. Like hey, look at me, I'm not who you remember me as.

But *I am*. I am the exact same person you met when you were a kid. I'm that same person you fell in love with. I know years and traumas and probably PTSD got into the way but it's *me*. Maybe my personality has changed and maybe I left some scars on you, but at least my heart is the same, and my heart loves you.

Sometimes, I don't think you understand that in order to love someone you have to love the bad traits about them too. You don't stop fighting for them, you don't run away when the going gets tough. You stick around, you search for all the reasons you loved that person to begin with.

I am tired of acting all tough. I am tired of taking two steps forward and five back because you're having an inner conflict and you can't decide who and what you want.

But I know your heart and that's what kills me. I know your heart. And I know you and I know how much you love me.

Hearts are like atoms, and I always said that if I believed deep down in my heart you no longer loved me, I will walk away and cut all ties of hope. But like atoms, I'm vibrating because you are, no matter where you are and who you're with.

Maybe our story hasn't ended yet. Maybe we have so much more to get through and to learn from and to move past and to love despite.

But knowing you, putting effort and standing ground for what you love is not a thing.

Love is a war that you have no intention of entering.

You're too weak to actually understand what love is, you're too cowardly.

You might escape everything now, avoid everything, take the easy route, please anyone by doing the bare minimum, by being selfish, by avoiding promises to make sure your conscious doesn't get affected.

If the pain I'm going through is to repent for something I did, I will happily suffer through it until the odds are even. And your turn will come and I know for a fact that all my prayers will be answered too.

I hope when the day comes, you'll be strong enough to go through it.

# Letting You Go

I guess I knew a while ago that it was the beginning of the end. As much as I refused to believe it, I believed it. the pain lingered deep down in my heart and it devoured my emotions day by day, hoping, just hoping that I was wrong.

But I wasn't.

I knew there would come a breaking point that will break us. something that will completely set us apart. No matter how big or small, one day, one of us will finally decide that what's going on is simply too much to handle.

One day, one of us will fall out of love while the other remains in pain of loving too much.

It was inevitable, we saw it coming but we didn't have reasons to finally call things off, once and for all. We didn't have the strength, we didn't want to be accountable or filled with guilt of being the ones who let go.

One of us would've had to leave with the blame of shattering things to the point they were unfixable.

I gave you the reason and you had the chance you were waiting for.

So I took the blame, with remorse and a broken heart, I took it.

And I gave you the one-way ticket out of my life you were hoping to get.

# 3 AM

It was around 3 am when I heard my phone buzz. Being the light-sleeper that you knew I was, I immediately awoke.

Before even checking the Caller ID, I had a feeling deep down in my gut that it was you. You see, no matter where you are or how far away you are from me, I can always feel and sense you around me. I know. I always know it's you. You can never truly stop a loving heart from knowing.

I picked up the phone call and for minutes on end, you said nothing whilst I heard your deep breaths on the other end of the line. Oh, that breath of yours I was in agony of hearing.

We both said nothing and perhaps had ended up sleeping whilst still on the phone. I really don't know.

The next morning, it was as if it was all just a dream. I haven't heard from you since and I hope to God that everything is alright with you.

You see, I'd never come after you with *whys* and *hows* and what made you call; I made a promise to you three years ago that is still standing today. I promised I'd be here no matter what.

And I was there for you, at 3 am, when all you needed for comfort was the sound of my breath and knowing I was with you.

I guess that's what hurts the most, knowing I can never truly walk away from you no matter how badly you broke me. I'll always be there. And you know it.

# Are You Here for Me?

you're back, not to my surprise
with all the love I begged to have
came so late, or early?
is it meant to save me from the present?
help me dodge a bullet?
are you my savior? or a demon in disguise?

are you here for me?
or for your selfish needs?

I need clarity
I need your words to stop sounding
like poison, like lies and disloyalty
I need it to sound true
honest, like the love I know I have
for you, and you have for me
but I can't help but feel like a burden
like I'm merely *not good enough*
like I'm replaceable, temporary
what is happening?
I'm drowning in confusion
why does love look like this

dressed up in a nightmare
shades of black pouring out
of a little organ impersonating a heart
why does pain seem
like collateral damage
to the entire picture?
are you here for me?
are you listening?

# Quarantine

I'm fine, thanks for asking
although I know deep down
you don't really care
stalking became a habit
to check on my whereabouts
and updates, seeing how much
I am now better without you.

I'm fine, thanks for asking
the virus didn't catch me
and I'm still alive
despite my toxic family
stress from university
loss of appetite
depression and anxiety
I'm keeping it together.

I'm not fine, thanks for 'asking'
you should've asked
when you had nothing to gain
when I was in pain

looking for a will
to live again
without you.

but I'm fine, thanks for asking.

# My Dearest

my dearest…
I have fed you love
for a decade
until you flourished
I've given you the sun
and moon
at the palm of your hands
I chased off your nightmares
and let your dreams linger
I've adopted insomnia
from your sleepless nights
my darling
I cheered you on
during your milestones
successes and achievements
I wiped your tears
and carried your burdens as mine.

my love
I dimmed my light to shine yours
why was it never good enough?

# I Don't Want to Bother You

I don't want to bother you
with this or that
with what's going on
and how I'm feeling
the pain that's devouring me
is none of your concern
I know now, I know well
where we stand
and where we'll go
this is the beginning
of the end
that we all saw coming
yet refused to believe
I knew then
like I know now
when you shut me down
discard me
invalidate my emotions
relinquish my heart

I was so blinded by you
and us, and all of it;
the package of constant
torment and agony.

so I don't want to bother you
with this or that
and what's going on
and how I am feeling
the pain is my concern
and I know now, I know well
this is all a masquerade
of fraudulent love
with your true colors
shining as my light dimmed
I believe now like I believed then
you always shut me down
I am always discarded
never enough
never wanted
the package of manipulation
and distrust.

so I don't want to bother you
ever again
with this or that
and how I'm feeling.

# Look at Me

look at me!

look at me!

I'm that girl you've always wanted
blonde hair, brown eyes
silk smooth body
curves and edges
a loving heart
kind, patient and tolerant.

look at me!

I'm in your dreams and fantasies
dressed in a satin gown
waiting at the aisle
look at me
I'm everything you ever wished for
everything you hoped
to have, to hold, to love.

so why are you still looking for me in someone else?

# Dec 2020

this was different
this was different than
the usual flings, hook-ups
every sin in the book
every lust-filled dream
you were a reality
amongst the darkness
you were the light
beaming through the clouds
subtly, softly, giving
me life. Satisfying my hunger
in small doses, quenching
my thirst with intimate drops
hold my hand, baby
I'm internally cold
I need your warmth
I need your soft lips on mine
I need your breath against my skin
hold my hand, baby
stare deep into my eyes
tell me this is a lie
a mere dream of forbidden lust

forbidden love
forbidden touch
I'm craving you now
more than ever, I need
your hands on mine so
"hold my hands, baby
it's cold outside."

# The Corner of Belgravia

just off the corner of Belgravia
I fell in love with your eyes
as you pulled me by my waist
and put your hands ever so
delicately, on the back of my neck
my mind played Louis Armstrong
and Frank Sinatra
as your scent warmed up my soul
I was waiting for you
little did I know you would revive me
bring me back to life
spark my senses, make me
love life, and you
and life with you
welcome home, honey
let my heart embrace you the way
my arms and eyes do
let me show you the rainbows
life offers, and the shooting stars
as we make our wishes of a better
future, and present
as we erase our miserable pasts

let me love you the way I have never before
and trace your scars as I feel
them healing right below
my fingertips, let me admire
your pain and aches and make them
my map towards an eternity with you.

just off the corner of Belgravia
I fell in love with you.

# Emotionally Unavailable

I'm not emotionally available
I cannot be yours forever
or even now
I'm not your happy ending
I'm not your fairytale
or princess in disguise
I cannot be held
within your hopes of compassion
you cannot save me
from this fallen angel
that lives within me
that has me shackled
in his hell of desire
I cannot be yours
as long as I breathe
my fiery lungs are filled
with his toxicity
my woeful heart has been
caught captive, in his bloody
hands, in his unfaithful heart
I cannot be yours
listen to what I'm saying

I'm a prisoner amongst the free
I live a gruesome horror
I breathe fear and pain
I cannot be yours
I cannot be yours
he owns my heart
he has my heinous life
he tortures my loving him.

and I cannot be yours
you cannot save me
from my fallen angel
that I'll love
until hell freezes over.

# One Second

you know what hurts the most?
the sudden sadness
after the ecstatic high
the falling so hard
when you least expect it
like one second you're
dancing and floating
on top of a rainbow
and the next
you are down
so below
that it makes you feel numb
you sit there staring
at the blankness
of a dark fog
and the flashbacks of pain
shower your eyes with tears
that refuse to fall down
so they burn for a while
as you witness everything
that destroyed you
for the thousandth time

and you experience it
again
and again
every once in a while
just to remind you
of how far you didn't go
of the ten steps you took forward
that took you twenty back
that one moment
that changed everything
where everything crashed
and broke and tore and
burned but still
the ashes choke you
when you least expect it
and you just sit there
waiting for the fog to pass
and to go back
to your life after the trauma
while still being stuck in it
because that one moment
wrecks it all
and you're back to square one
hoping this time, your high
lasts a little longer
and the low won't kill you
that this time
you'll actually feel stronger

and the tears won't burn you
that this time
it'll be a mere memory
that won't ever haunt you.

# Victim

I thought the pain ended
when I rolled over
and kissed your face
while you're asleep
I thought the pain ended
when you promised me
a new beginning
a new life, free of disappointments
and betrayal
and a better tomorrow
I thought this was my chance
that it was now or never
to claim you back
to take us back
to unite despite the aching
to replenish the emptiness
to build what you broke
I thought I deserved this
for once and finally
to have you in my arms
solely mine, now
and forever

I thought despite it all
you were mine, you are mine
that your heart was waiting
for me to wake it up
that you stood there
waiting for me
waiting for us
I thought no one
made a home out of you
I thought no matter what
I was your home
your solace
your muse.

what fantasy I lived in
my little pink fairyland
thinking I deserved happiness
thinking I claimed you forever
thinking nothing would change
within your past
and present
and future
but betrayal lingers within
your impurity and conniving nature.

and I was your victim
yet again…
yet again.

# Second Choice

I'm always going to be
the second choice
second best
second…overall
never perfect for you
but just good enough
to give you the satisfaction
the ultimate high, *temporarily*
the one you call at 2 am
for a quickie,
you lay in my bed
after you've pleasured
yourself in my body
you curl up my hair
around your fingertips
as I rest my head
on your chest; my home
telling me you love me
but you look away
and I almost hear her name
instead of mine
in between the lines

of what little you say to me
in the heaviness of your breath
and the cracks in your voice
her, within every sentence
you almost slip up
I almost hear it
and I listen ever so closely
waiting…

but you never do
you keep her tucked in
between your ribcage
somewhat sacred
away from me and my doubts
and I'm the one
kept in secret
late night visits, hidden
from unwanted eyes
in fear of anyone
knowing what you're doing
and I welcome you each time
open arms, surrendering
to this lust-based
lack of a relationship…

you'd think I'd be the one
but I'd never be
I'm just *good enough*
the one that listens
and forgives
the one that never

asks any questions
avoids conflicts, lets
you come and go as
you please
every time you wash yourself
off of me, and shut the door
the pain of knowing
what I know
and yet another night
you curl up my hair
around your fingers
and look away as you
tell me you love me.

and I almost hear her name
I almost hear her name.

# The Dews

sometimes, I miss
the dews on the grass
during the cold early mornings
how the fog stains
the windows, like a curtain
blocking off hope
until you step out into
the thick air, waiting for it
to clear out
I put the coffee pot
on the stove
and heard it sizzling
I made my bed
all whilst looking at the window
every once in a while
desperate for the sun to beam through
I forgot your face
and today felt oddly unusual
weren't you here last night?
before the rise broke out
before the birds chirped
weren't you here before

the crack of dawn?
I forgot what your presence
feels like, your perfume
and the shade of your
favorite sweater
I poured my coffee into the cup
and stepped out beyond the window
I sat down and looked over
the fog started clearing out
the dews were disappearing
I couldn't seem to remember your face
weren't you here last night?

# Blood and Wine

it broke
the glass broke
the one with red wine
the rug is stained in shades
of purple and red
a hint of blue, I don't know
I'm gonna have to clean
this up, it's bothering me
almost like a murder scene
before the police rush in
and tape the areas in yellow
I don't know how we got here
what you said before the shattering
did you hurt yourself, my dear?
show me your hands
I can't tell what's blood from the wine
what's wrong from the right
I'm starting to lose my balance
can you hold on to me
tell me how we got here
tell me how you broke the glass
with your bare hands?

tell me how furious you are at me
tell me I am worthless
and how much you hate me
and all the pain I caused
yell and scream and hit me.

I can't keep doing this anymore
the broken hearts and broken glasses
I can't clean them up.

# Against My Will

I'm getting tired of it all
my heart is giving up slowly
it's not that I can't stand tall
but you're treating me coldly.

I tried to manifest the strength
I tried to look past it all
but sometimes, the breakup's length
makes things clash and fall.

your lies and betrayal don't seem to end
it's me and her and her and her
I thought I could do it and not mend
my rules for you and what we were.

despite it all, I thought it through
it's hard to say, it's very hard still
that you and I are no longer due…
that you'll always go against my will.

# I'm Sorry

I don't know how to say this
I'm scared of breaking your heart
I don't think I carry love for you
and I'm unsure where to start.

it might've been the distance
or the resentment and falling apart
but sometimes, I wonder if at all
I wanted you gone to restart.

I'm really sorry I no longer can
be the one that forever stands
I can't be your all-time muse
and I promise you, this was unplanned.

in the end, I hope you can forgive
all the love I failed to understand
I know I've been a toxic hell
I hope this pain you can withstand.

"I don't think we should be together,"
he said as he carried my heart and left.

"I don't want to be with you anymore, I really don't. I don't think this can work. Please don't get mad at me, I know this isn't what you wanted to hear. I really tried...I tried to love you again. I couldn't. I know I'm failing you and setting fire to our dreams...what else can I do though? I wanted to give you everything you ever wanted. I know I promised you the galaxies and the universe. I wish I hadn't. You see, I can never seem to keep my promises. I always find a way to break them. I always disappoint, never meet anyone's expectations. But that's on me. I wish I still loved you the way I used to, but I don't," he mumbled with little specks of sweat trickling from his forehead. "Please, say something, please, anything."

"But what can I say? I've heard all of this before. From men that don't look like you but behave the same...It's always the same shit, isn't it? I'm fucking tired. Just go."

# The Promise

I'm not sure what hurts the most
the fact that I'm not allowed to get close
or the fact that I can't walk away
I'm sorry, I've been harsh on you
I don't think I meant it, or maybe I did
I don't want to blame it on my emotions
at the time, maybe I wanted to hurt you too
I went through a lot, some of it you know about
a lot that was hidden
I didn't mean to turn us into ashes
but I felt I was forced to
my life feels like sand dunes
I'm struggling to climb them
but when I do, sliding down is easy
maybe this is what healing feels like
soft sand dunes under the bright sun
exhausting, but you find relief at the end
I wasn't sure I'd see the light
at the end of the very long tunnel
or maybe I thought you'd be there

waiting for me to reach
to apologize and make amends
but the light was waiting, like the promise is
that everything will be okay
I just didn't think everything will be okay without you.

# Unfaithful

I shouldn't have given you
my number, my attention
I should've walked away
remained loyal
faithful, trapped in my
failing relationship
I couldn't fight the urge
you were simply too charming
until I got to see you, for you
that's when I knew
you were more than an attractive
face, you were my dream,
knight in shining armor
everything I had hoped for
right before my eyes
you completed me
you entered my heart and soul
no questions asked
without knocking
you stole my breath away
I was enchanted
hell, might've even fallen in love

this is all a mistake
and I don't want it to end
to stop
I'm sorry you're not my first
I'm sorry, I'm not available
forgive me
I will burn the world
for you, to be with you
I will fight against my odds
I want you
I will make it happen
screw who gets hurt
this is love
I've been waiting for this
this is love.

I shouldn't have given you
my attention
but fuck it, you stole it anyway.

# I Can't Explain

I know you're furious at me
livid, angry, frustrated
I know you're fighting hard
the urge to knock off the wall behind me
or maybe just even strangle me
and feel me losing my breath
in between your hands
I don't want to apologize for what I did
I was hurt, I am hurt
and although I forgave you
it's always hard to forget
it haunts me sometimes, the way
you left…the way I died
this slow death each day
that you were gone
you never allowed me the closure
and I'm with you again having
not healed fully, the trauma
is simply too vivid and present
you don't know the days I get triggered
and I sit on my bed rereading every text
the words flow on messages

like bloodstains of my broken heart
every word of every text
creates new wounds upon the old
like daggers into my soul
like knives carving out my heart
slowly, as if to create a masterpiece
as if to inflict torment
it's an excruciating pain I cannot
begin to explain…I can't
put into words or poems
all my suffering, it's unbearable
you wouldn't handle it
I'm sorry that you'd hate yourself
if you knew, but you have to know.

apart from the heartbreak
which isn't seen on movies
it wasn't tears wept, more like bloodsheds
and days and nights go on
as I feel my body drying out
of blood, of power, of emotions
the life in me slowly fading
and yet, I chose to come back
running, forgiving, welcoming
I loved you, it was my only option
to rescue what was left,
to put out the raging fire, I had to
brush my feelings under the rug
hoping it wouldn't resurface
but here we are today
back to where it all started

the nagging and bickering
the game of breaking hearts
that you excel and I try
like a broken puppet you push me around
and I break each time you do
and maybe I'm not making sense
but how can I explain
so I try to show you a little
of what I went through, and I'm sorry
to put you through a fraction of it
I'm sorry you don't understand
why I do what I do, why I insist
on making you suffer
please forgive me, I want you to know
what it feels like to be discarded
the second option, the unwanted
call it coping mechanism
walls built up high, trust issues
call me cold-hearted and ruthless.

but I can't explain
so I show you a little.

I didn't want you back…matter of fact, I didn't want anything to do with you at all. All I wanted was for the suffering to end, the wounds to heal and the pain to be forgotten. Yet…you were so persistent on staying in my life, constantly leaving and coming back after long lengths of time, causing more loathing and disgust, thinking it will somehow rekindle my love for you when in reality, it gave me more and more reasons to hate you.

To think, I might come back running to you, sweetie, how delusional can you be? Even the weakest woman can manage to create strength that overpowers her own heart when it comes to heartbreak and, honey, you didn't just create a void in my heart, you dug your own grave.

# Untrustworthy

I should've known not to trust this
a beautiful lie can only deceive so much
before the truths burn bright
to say I was blinded by love
is an understatement, I was deafened too
I carried a love for you so big
it covered the cruelty of the universe
it surpassed all the shooting stars
I thought carried your name
and I prayed for you to the heavens;
oh please, let me have this one
I have sinned and I beg for mercy
I plead, don't punish me with him
I am exhausted, I treaded the world
cuffed by the ankle by hope
of a happy ever-after
I swam the oceans and drowned
a million deaths each time
looking for an eternal shore
and yet another shooting star

passes by tonight, carrying your name
and I pray to the heavens
oh please, I beg
let me have this one
let me have this one.

# Out of the Blue

you really hurt me
and I wonder why you think
I cry out of the blue sometimes
or why I scream your name
into the darkness
and it takes me back to the day
you left me running around
in circles, trying to find out
where you went and with who
it's never out of the blue
it's as constant as my slow breaths
and my beating heart
this pain that never seems to leave
persisting, gnaws at my soul
I never pitied myself before
but now feeling pathetic
became my middle name
as I witness you drift away yet again
I know the signs now, the symptoms
of cheating, I can easily spot them
it all starts with small talk
that get less and less each day

you slowly start hating my voice
and the way I say your name
I'm no longer worth explanations
or apologies or respect
someone else replaces me
I know the symptoms
I know the effects.

# Déjà Vu

it's past 3 on a Tuesday
I know you're not up to much
the days are slow
you're probably on bed
texting a new her
this all feels familiar now
you haven't asked to see me
in ages, or spoken to me
and I know you no longer look
at my pictures
I forgot your phone number
just like I've forgotten your voice
you no longer even bother
with small talk, a bunch of
*hi*s and *hello*s, as empty
as your feelings towards me
people call this Déjà Vu
when you feel as though
you've experienced this before

but this time
it isn't a feeling
I know what you're up to
I know where this will go
it's all too familiar

# Video Games

you have all my switches
buttons, you know
how and when to trigger me
shut me down again
make me your play toy
you constantly play
make believe house
with me, painting a fake picture
of rainbows and golden
sunshine, then you rip
that picture into pieces
like you do with my heart
at the end of every night
that game turns off
and I'm back to laying in my bed
all alone, wondering if what happened
was reality or a delusion
of you and I.

I think the worst part of watching you outgrow me was witnessing how much you're growing to like all the things I've always wanted you to like, but you weren't liking them for me, you liked them for someone else.

# Love Triangle

I've always heard of the chaos
of having two people
each one at the end
of a very sharp triangle
you must pick and choose,
right? you must decide
who is it that you want.
I wanted you, long ago
from the very beginning
always been you, 2 years and counting
but fate brought someone
in between
that disrupted the peace we had
you never showed me any interest
or said a word about your feelings
your eyes never lingered on mine
and your fingers never found their way
towards my hands, the way he does
yet I wanted you so desperately
so I tried to show you
little did I know he would come after me
so fiercely so abruptly
standing on top of a cliff

yelling at the top of his lungs
"I want you"
and all I can murmur in between
the tears burning my cheeks
"but I want him.
I want him."

# Trust Issues

you knew I had trust issues
I told you, one night,
during a long phone call
I've been betrayed, cheated on
I've tolerated more than my heart
could ever handle
it has broken me to pieces
and I'm still struggling
to put back what is scattered
I showed you the darkness
that lives within me
and all the agony and pain
the cold rivers in my veins
that run through me carrying
all the bitterness in this world.
I told you what it is like
to feel second best, insecure
not good enough,
yet you held my hands and
promised me kindness
waterfalls of warm care
to wash away the ruinous rivers

and I believed you…
like I've never believed anyone
and that is the danger of love
every birth of tenderness
the intensity of attachment
makes you forget all the exertion
you've put your heart through
the promise of an everlasting fondness
the promise of fraud loyalty
the promise of forever
is a mere deceiving hallucination
I was too blind to see
I was too blind to care
I craved your love like it was
the last antidote to heartbreak
like it was the last cloud
carrying rain to wash me
out of all I've known
I saw all your red lights
as blinking orange
and I sped through hoping
just hoping I wouldn't miss my chance
and if I crashed oh well
I knew the consequences
and I thought the risk is worth it all
but like that last cloud of rain
you left my skies
and rained on a different city
where the sun shines afterward

just a little brighter
for you and her, by a river stream
where there are no flowers
because how can a flower grow
when cold rivers wash them away?

# Memories

your memories devour me
through the gloominess of long nights
consuming all of my thoughts
and all of my being
taking my soul toward you
flying me over, like a breeze
like on clouds with wings on my back
just to be with you
and I want you.
here, with me, forever.
I want to feel your touch
and your breath against my skin
I want your lips on mine
and your hands between my thighs
memories aren't enough to suffice
I need you within me, in me
and all it means to be in your presence
I want the darkness to come from your rage
as you tell me you miss me
and slam me against the wall
I want your hands on my neck
demanding I choke "I'm yours"

but it's just one of those nights
where your memories devour me
and all I can do is patiently wait
until we're reunited again.

# To You, for You

many years ago I found you
only person that caught my attention
having been through life without you
and trying to reach my book ascension
maybe you'll find yourself amongst my words
maybe you'll even try to ignore
even if you walk further than toward
day by day I loved you more

lonely I've been since you left
occasionally, I'd write to express
or to let my feelings be known
to find my inner peace and self
and to everything that was unknown
here's my book on your shelf

# Blinks of Orange

it's around 4:30 am I think
they just turned off the lights on the street
the sun is about to rise soon
although your light is still missing
the air feels thick and humid
just another summer morning
nothing really feels odd
or out of place, although I know I am
I started sitting in the balcony
waiting for the sunrise, something I never did before
I was always a sunset person, I shared them with you
but now sitting waiting for a new day became my glimpse of
hope
although I'm not sure what hope is to come if I'm up all
night
I stare at the street lights and I memorized how long it takes
for them to turn red to green
about a couple minutes or so
and with every blink of orange
the wait, the patience, the rush
either or, that's when my feelings get lethargic
I think my life is stuck at an orange blink

I'm not gone and I'm not stopped, I'm always in the middle
I know it's about time to move on yet something keeps me
here
it's like watching the sunrise because I haven't slept all night
not because I woke up to appreciate it
I can't seem to go or come back or whatever it is I have to
do

I'm just stuck in the middle
like orange blinks on a street light.

# Street Lights

again, same timing, its 4:32
this time I'm not on the balcony
I'm sitting in the middle of the street
there's a certain thrill about laying down here
just waiting for the lights to go from red to green
just like they do in "The Notebook"
although my story doesn't end like Noah and Allie
there is no happy ever after, no unconditional love
the green has passed and we're back at the orange
and I remember your face
your voice
your touch
oh I'm so scared of forgetting you, of my mind betraying me
the way you betrayed my heart and soul
I feel as though I'm not laying down
I'm scattered
I'm no longer weak at the knees just like the day I walked to
you at the airport
I'm broken in pieces beyond repair thrown in the gravel and
concrete
the trauma replays itself every time
the lies after lies, the manipulation and betrayal

the never-ending cycle of grief
the way you said goodbye and kissed me with a promise
you'd come back
the way you walked down the aisle on my birthday hand in
hand with someone else
the deception, your perfidy nature
oh how did I ever fall in love, how was I so goddamned
blind
your eyes were trying to tell me the truth date after date
all whilst I thought it was the stars and moon shining
through
I'm weak now look at me look into my eyes
they burn and burn and burn but no tears want to disperse
I'm trapped and I want to move on, I so badly want to
the green light comes and passes and I'm stopped
I'm stopped.
I'm stopped.
I'm prisoned.
I'm cuffed.
I'm detained by all the lakes and oceans we once loved
and all the I love yous between our kisses
and all the dreams and hopes of an eternity together

but the green light comes and goes
and I'm still in the gravel.